SPOTLIGHT ON THE RISE AND FALL OF ANCIENT CIVILIZATIONS™

ANCIENT MESOPOTAMIAN DAILY LIFE

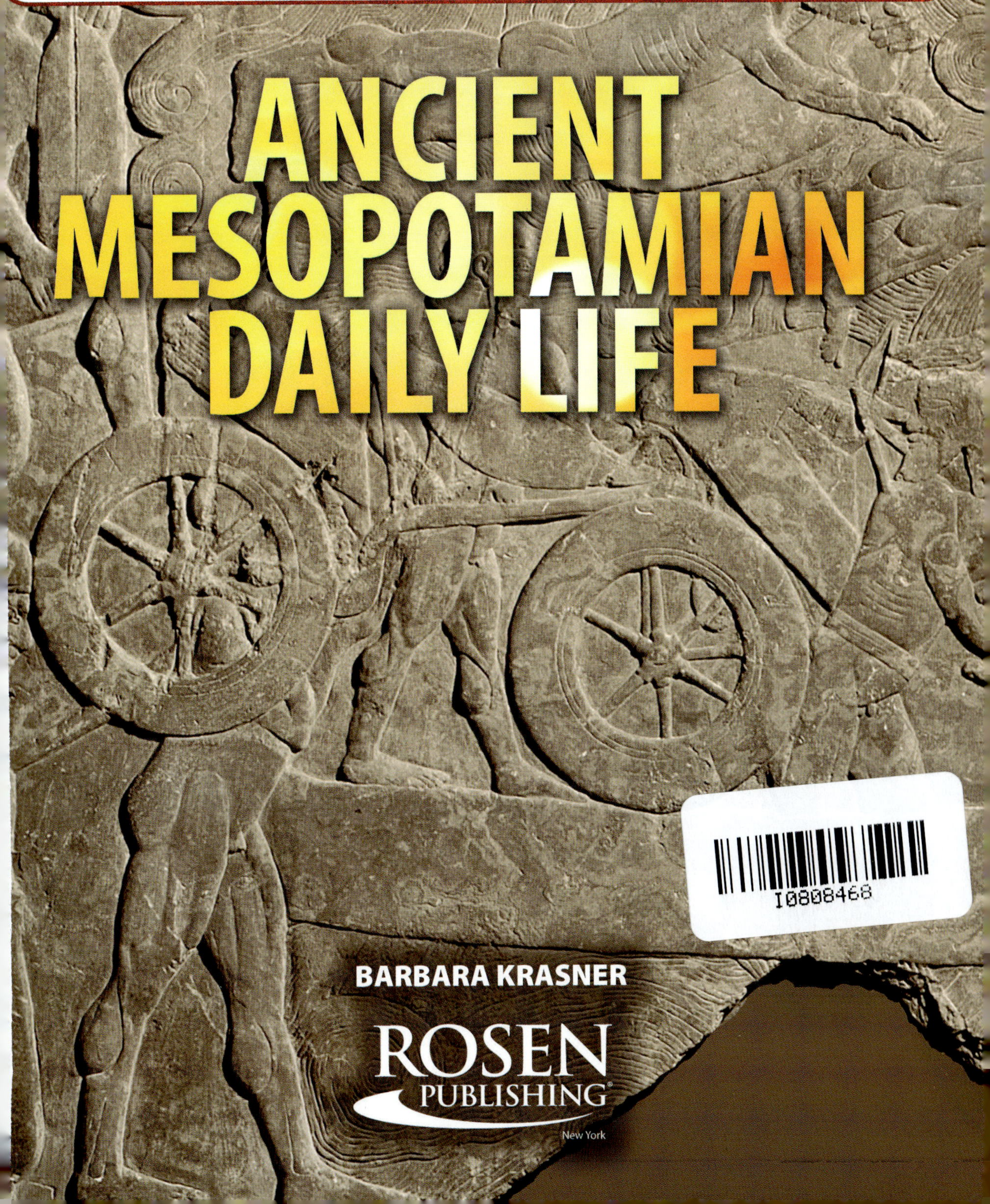

BARBARA KRASNER

ROSEN PUBLISHING
New York

Published in 2017 by The Rosen Publishing Group, Inc.
29 East 21st Street, New York, NY 10010

First Edition

Library of Congress Cataloging-in-Publication Data

Names: Krasner, Barbara.
Title: Ancient Mesopotamian daily life / Barbara Krasner.
Description: First edition. | New York : Rosen Publishing, 2017. | Series: Spotlight on the rise and fall of ancient civilizations | Includes bibliographical references and index.
Identifiers: LCCN 2016003298| ISBN 9781477789070 (library bound) | ISBN 9781477789056 (paperback) | ISBN 9781477789063 (6-pack)
Subjects: LCSH: Iraq—History—To 634—Juvenile literature. | Iraq—Social life and customs—Juvenile literature. | Middle East—History—To 622—Juvenile literature. | Middle East—Social life and customs—Juvenile literature.
Classification: LCC DS71 .K695 2017 | DDC 935—dc23
LC record available at http://lccn.loc.gov/2016003298

Manufactured in the United States of America

CONTENTS

WHERE IN THE WORLD WAS MESOPOTAMIA?

The name *Mesopotamia* comes from the ancient Greek and means "land between the rivers." Mesopotamia was located between the Tigris and Euphrates Rivers, occupying the land of present-day Iraq, Syria, Kuwait, and southeastern Turkey. Mesopotamia included the cities of Nineveh, Ur, and Assur, and included the regions of Assyria, Babylonia, Akkadia, and Sumer. Assyria lay to the north; Babylonia and Sumer lay to the south; and Akkadia was in the middle.

Mesopotamia earned its reputation as the cradle of civilization. It produced the world's first writing system. It also gave birth to the world's first cities. Mesopotamia was made up of a collection of cultures with regional differences. There was a social class system, too, and people living in the cities had different experiences from those in more rural areas. Information about the rhythm of daily lives of Mesopotamians comes from recovered clay tablets, Greek texts, and the Bible.

Mesopotamia held a significant and strategic position between the Tigris and Euphrates Rivers. It covered present-day Iraq, Syria, Kuwait, and part of Turkey.

OF CODES AND CLASS

King Hammurabi, who reigned from 1792 to 1750 BCE, established a set of laws in his first year as ruler. The Code of Hammurabi directed the Mesopotamians' daily lives. For example, these laws outlined punishments for crimes. Kings used these laws to help them decide how to treat those who committed crimes. When a man broke the law, he might have been punished severely, even with death.

Wealth dictated placement in Mesopotamia's social structure. Owning property, in particular, placed one higher in the social order than having money but no property.

The Code of Hammurabi mentioned three social classes. An *awīlum* was a gentlemen free of any debt. A *muškēnum* was a poor man. A *wardum* was a slave. The good news was that if a man was born a slave, he could be freed. However, a free man could go into debt. Still, a man could change the class he was born into.

The Code of Hammurabi outlined punishments if Mesopotamians did not follow the laws. Here, an Assyrian artist showed King Hammurabi receiving the laws from the sun god Shamash.

VILLAGE COMMUNITIES AND THE ROAMING NOMADS

Farming in ancient Mesopotamia was a major part of daily life, especially in the villages that dotted the countryside. The village structure enabled people to stay in one place. They constructed dwellings. Villages governed themselves in ancient Mesopotamia. Villages, more common in the north than in the south, tended to be the property of the king or a wealthy overlord. Many city residents owned property in the country. Some villages grew to the size of cities once agriculture and irrigation were mastered.

Nomads, or shepherds, roamed with their herds. They belonged to tribes or clans. These were groups that included many families. Men from these tribes found employment as agricultural workers or laborers. They also served as soldiers. Their migrations in search of grazing land for their animals made them ideally suited to be traders also. At times, they controlled the trade routes between Mesopotamia and the West.

Urban dwellers considered nomads to be uncivilized.

Ancient Mesopotamians lived in villages like the one modeled here. For many, the village formed the center of daily life.

WITHIN CITY WALLS

Cities became a part of Mesopotamian daily life as early as 4000 BCE. Archaeologists have estimated that a Mesopotamian city could have had between ten thousand and one hundred thousand people.

Cities had exterior walls. Within these walls were temples, royal palaces, and homes. Outside the walls was the suburb, an outer city, which had homes, farms, and fields. It furnished the city with food and materials.

Cities rose up along the rivers, which, along with canals, provided drinking water. The wharf was the center of commerce, and foreign traders established stores there. Some cities became distinguished by certain features, such as Asshur's location on a cliff and Borsippa, which straddled two lakes.

Most cities were not prosperous. Their economy depended on the king's victories. War brought wealth.

The real power in the city belonged to the king and the people he favored.

Exterior walls were built around cities like Babylonia, shown here, to protect them from enemy invasions. Babylonia's wall was made of brick and was 56 miles (90 kilometers) long.

INSIDE THE HOME

Housing and furnishings used by ancient Mesopotamians every day varied by time period, location, and the owners' wealth. In general, houses provided shelter from twelve hours of unrelenting summer heat. They were made of mud brick, which in turn was made of clay and straw. Walls were made of mud plaster, roofs of mud and poplar, and doors of wood. Bitumen and lime plaster waterproofed the lower parts of the walls.

Furniture was made of wood, and leather provided the upholstery. Chairs came in all shapes and sizes. Some were highly decorated with griffins and winged animals. Beds were stuffed with wool and goat's hair. The poor, however, slept on straw or reed mats.

Household goods included containers for storage, such as baskets, skins, clay bins, wooden chests, crates, and jars. To eat and drink, Mesopotamians used ladles, single-pointed bone forks, bronze or iron knives, platters, bowls, and cups. They also ate out of ostrich eggshells.

This example of a royal Sumerian plate dates back to 2000 BCE. It is made of clay, and at its center is a design featuring wild goats.

ALL IN THE FAMILY

To ancient Mesopotamians, a typical house was occupied by a married couple and their children. A man had only one wife, and he was expected to build a house. If his wife could not bear children, he could take a second wife or a concubine, or they could adopt. On average, from two to four children survived early childhood. Other family members sometimes lived with the family unit. These family members might have included unmarried sisters, widowed mothers, and young brothers.

In the home, the father ruled. If a son struck his father, his hand would be cut off, as dictated by the Code of Hammurabi.

Men were known by their fathers' names. In the first millennium BCE, a free man was called by his given name, followed by his father's name, and then followed by his ancestor's name, who would likely have been his grandfather or another important ancestor: X, son of Y, descendant of Z. Slaves did not have family names.

The Code of Hammurabi, a portion of which is shown here, also dictated punishments for family members who mistreated each other.

THE SPOKEN AND WRITTEN WORD

Ancient Mesopotamians spoke a variety of languages. No one knows the first spoken language in Mesopotamia, but the first recorded language was Sumerian, a language unrelated to any other. To the south, in Sumer, people started speaking Sumerian around 3100 BCE. It was spoken for two thousand years. It is considered a classical language, like Latin and Greek.

The Akkadians brought their Semitic language to northern and central Mesopotamia in the third millennium BCE. It relied on three letters as the root of each word. Akkadian became the major Mesopotamian language in the second millennium BCE. It became the language of business, trade, and negotiation between nations. It had two dialects: Babylonian in the south and Assyrian in the north.

Aramaic, another Semitic language, replaced Akkadian in the first millennium BCE. Introduced by the Amorites, Aramaic became the major language of the Near East.

The use of Aramaic became popular and replaced Akkadian in the first millennium BCE.

WHAT TO WEAR

Sumerian religious art depicts the use of sheepskins, goatskins, and fleeces for clothing for years. Once textiles became available, the most common material became wool.

Priests and other high-ranking religious officials wore fringed woolen dresses. Most popular among these dresses was the *kaunakes*, a long skirt of heavy wool. Kings wore garments that identified them as rulers, such as long tunics that resembled togas. They draped over the left shoulder, sometimes with decorative fringes. Kings also wore skullcaps.

The everyday man and woman wore a shorter draped robe or skirt, belted at the waist. Men wore sandals with wedges for heels. Women wore slippers.

Clothing styles changed in the first millennium BCE. Men wore short-sleeved, belted tunics. If a man was an administrative or military official, he might also have sported a cloak made of wool or linen.

Women wore headdresses and arranged their hair in chignons on both sides to keep the headdresses in place.

This female figure wears a *kaunakes* dress, a Sumerian garment made of wool. It was crafted in the area of modern-day Afghanistan.

SPARKLING GEMS AND OTHER JEWELRY

Since the seventh millennium BCE, shells, bones, and polished stones had been transformed into necklaces and bracelets. Wearing jewelry was an essential part of Mesopotamian daily life. Men, women, and children decorated themselves with gems and precious metals.

Most records of jewelry, however, are associated with royalty. Excavations of royal tombs from the first millennium BCE at Nimrud revealed hundreds of gold pieces, including a crown with marbled agate beads to ward off the evil eye. Queen Puabi's tomb of the third millennium BCE contained a lapis lazuli crown with golden animal, fruit, and flower decorations. Collar necklaces were made of gold, silver, lapis lazuli, carnelian, and agate.

Everyday people wore beads; necklaces; anklets; rings on their fingers, ears, and noses; and bracelets on their wrists and arms. They also wore amulets.

When their babies were born, mothers received jewelry. Jewelry was also given as wedding gifts. One generation passed down jewelry to the next at funerals.

Archaeologists uncovered Queen Puabi's magnificent headdress and jewelry from the Royal Tombs at Ur. They date back to 2600 BCE.

THE LONG AND SHORT OF HAIRSTYLES

In ancient Mesopotamia, the everyday hairstyle for men was long, reaching their shoulders and curled at the ends. They kept their hair in place with headbands of beads. Their beards were shaped.

Women also wore their hair long. They kept their hair in place with strands of beads, pendants, or flowers made of semiprecious stones. Sometimes, both men and women created small buns at the napes of their necks or braided their hair and tied it with rings of precious metal.

Some women's hairdos were quite elaborate. If a woman had a special hairdo, she probably also wore crescent-shaped earrings. Women were known to wear gold and silver hair ribbons. They also used gold ribbon hairnets and silver hairpins decorated with lapis lazuli (blue) and limestone (red) flowers.

Kings and priests typically shaved their heads. A bald head indicated a high position. Doctors and slaves also wore distinctive hairstyles that quickly identified them.

Gold ribbons and other hair ornaments were meant to beautify women's hair. Evidence of this came from excavations at the royal burial pits at Ur.

STRIKE UP THE BAND

Music played a vital role in daily ancient Mesopotamian life. Musicians played a variety of instruments. Percussion instruments included drums, cymbals, bells, pipes, and clappers. String instruments included the lyre, lute, and harp. These could have been highly decorated with lapis lazuli, mother of pearl, or ivory inlays. Wind instruments included bone, wood, or metal flutes and trumpets.

Musicians played at religious events, magic rituals, funerals, military events, and festivals. They also banged the drums at sporting events, such as boxing matches. They played hymns at temples and palaces. Sometimes, they played love songs, too.

Musicians had status in Mesopotamia. They were highly valued and were sometimes exchanged as prizes in war or as gifts between countries.

Mesopotamian music used a seven-note scale. Ancient tablets revealed the mechanics of making music. They named the strings of the lyre and the intervals between them. They also instructed how to tune the lyre to different keys.

A harp player accompanies his ruler, about 2500 BCE, on the popular Mesopotamian instrument.

TRAVELING BY SEA OR LAND

Cities were situated along the Tigris and Euphrates Rivers, which emptied into the Persian Gulf. But both rivers flowed north to south. That meant boats in ancient Mesopotamia could travel only south, with the current. The types of boats used included barges and ferries. They did not have rudders. One type of boat, the *kelek*, transported cargo. It used goatskins to stay afloat. Other boats used bitumen for waterproofing.

Man-made canals in the cities could also accommodate passenger and cargo boats.

To travel north, the trip had to be made by land. Travelers rode donkeys, and camels became efficient and popular for everyday travel around 1000 BCE. Donkeys pulled wheel-less sledges, and this was the preferred means of ground transportation even after the Sumerians invented the wheel. Two-wheel and four-wheel carts became available.

The Assyrians created a system of roads for their messengers. Messengers rode on horses, which were also used for ritual celebrations.

The *kelek* was a type of raft used to transport goods along the Tigris River. Goat skins helped the raft to float.

IN EXCHANGE

Mesopotamia was rich in agriculture because of the practice of irrigation. But it lacked many natural resources. Much had to be imported from other lands through invasion, overthrow, and trade. Mesopotamians bought tin, gold, silver, copper, ivory, and pearls from other parts of the Near East. From Africa, they imported gold, ebony, ivory, and carnelian. From the Middle East, they purchased timber and oils. They established trade links with the Indus Valley to the east for lapis lazuli and carnelian.

In exchange for these essentials, Mesopotamian traders offered crop surplus. Grains like barley, wheat, and sesame seeds as well as dates were traded. Textiles were also important to trade.

Merchants formed trade organizations and collaborated to operate trade caravans. Transactions took place mostly without money. Instead, traders used grain, gold, and silver. The Mesopotamian ability to write enabled them to record transactions with contracts, made official with a seal.

Ancient Mesopotamians used plentiful dates to trade for other goods. This was a profitable way for them to make good use of excess crops.

ALL IN A DAY'S WORK

Everyday people in Mesopotamia engaged in agriculture and crafts to earn their livings. Outside the city, the fields were fertile, and farmers grew crops. Soon they resulted in surplus, and the extra crops could be used to barter for other goods. That meant that not everyone needed to farm. They could instead specialize in a trade.

Weavers made cloths using looms, often in the home. Other craftsmen made baskets and vases. There were woodcutters and carpenters, boat makers and shoemakers. They worked with leather and metals. They cut stone. Some were skilled at butchering animals. Goldsmiths and silversmiths fashioned items of metal. A select number of skilled craftsmen were called upon to serve the needs of the palace.

Men were needed to dig and maintain city canals so the water would flow to the fields. There were architects, engineers, and bricklayers to plan and build the cities.

Artisans like goldsmiths and tinsmiths were called upon to make everyday and special occasion wares, such as this elaborate bowl.

PLAY THE GAME

Playing games was not only for fun and relaxation. It was linked to religion and rituals. Wrestling matches, for example, were held during religious rituals. Wrestlers fought without weapons or any other fighting aids.

Toys opened up a world of imagination for children. Boys could dream of future days of hunting and fighting when they played with miniature versions of weapons like slingshots, bows and arrows, and boomerangs. They also played with miniature carts, wagons, chariots, and ships. Other action-oriented toys and games included spinning tops, rattles, pucks and mallets, hoops, and balls. Girls could play house with miniature furniture, dolls, and animals. Children would play the game of Ishtar, a jump rope game.

Royal Mesopotamians had game boards placed in their tombs so when they were dead, they could play for eternity. The game boards were made of wood overlaid with shell, lapis lazuli, and limestone. Sets of squares covered the boards.

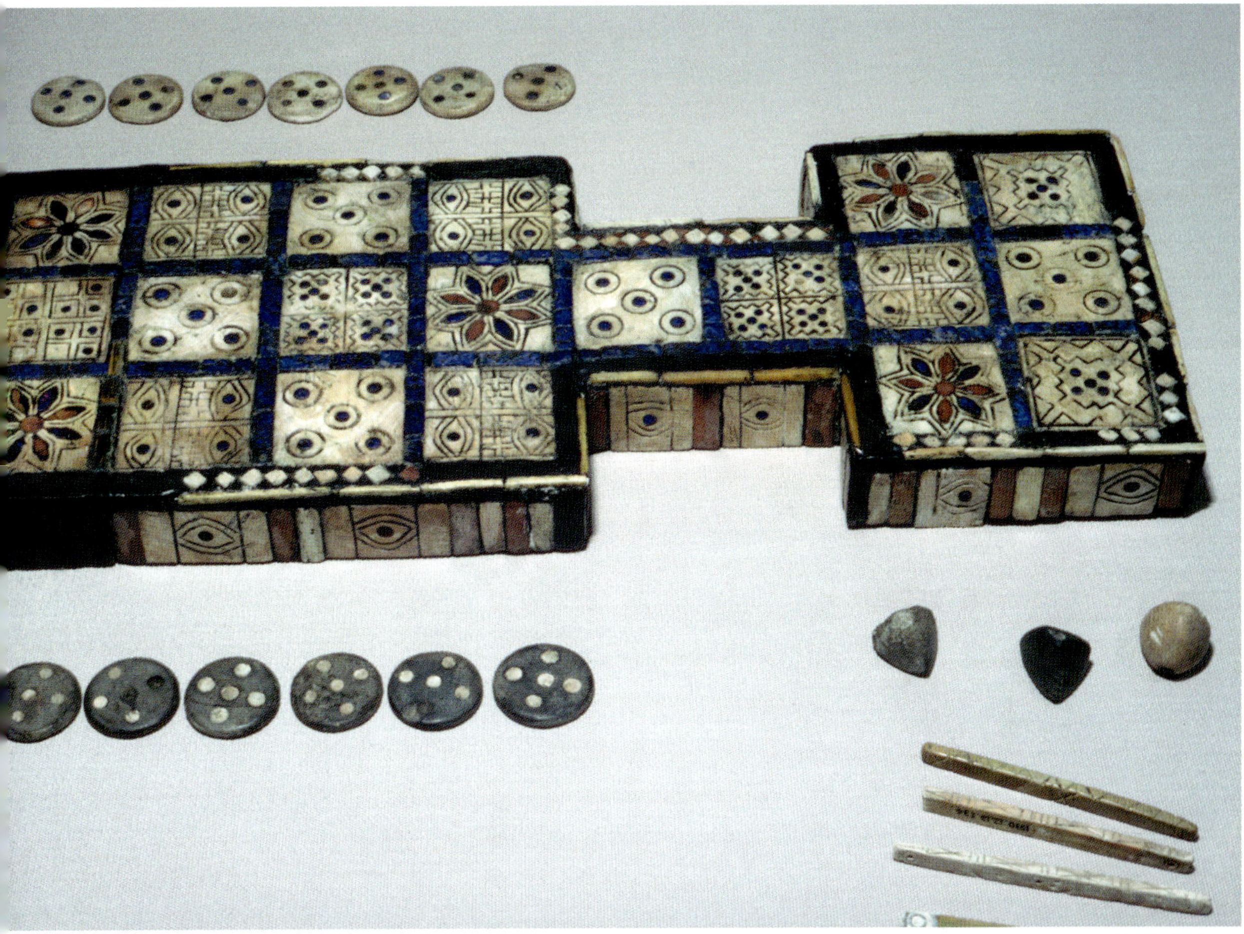

The Royal Game of Ur was discovered at the royal tombs there. Game boards were made of wood, shell, and jewels.

WAR!

Fighting wars was a way of life in ancient Mesopotamia. War determined who was king and the role of the city god. Enemies targeted the cities. Even with a city's walls and the city god for protection against attacks, if the city fell, so did the king's power.

The major weapon of war was the bow and arrow. But soldiers also used spears, daggers, and maces with stone heads. Soldiers received training in hand-to-hand combat. They knew how to box and wrestle. They rode in chariots and laid siege to enemy fortifications. There they used battering rams to attack.

To protect themselves, soldiers wore armor. Their armor included a helmet, and they held a shield.

Sumerian troops numbered in the thousands, and the Assyrians in the tens of thousands. The king or the people he chose led the troops into battle.

If a king lost a battle, ancient Mesopotamians believed the gods worked against him.

Armor, such as this Mesopotamian gold helmet from 2500 BCE, protected soldiers during military campaigns. The helmet is carved to look like hair.

WORSHIPPING MANY GODS

The Sumerians, Assyrians, and Babylonians gave their many gods different names, and their gods differed. But they all believed man's purpose was to serve the gods. The gods had a plan for mankind to follow. They controlled people's destinies and daily lives. Therefore, Mesopotamians believed in magical powers; they also believed that it was important to avoid the evil eye.

The gods included An or Anu, the king of the gods. Enlil or Ellil was second in authority to the king of gods and controlled the winds and the waters. Ishtar or Inanna was the goddess of love.

The Mesopotamians praised their gods with festivals, religious events, and banquets. In Babylon, people celebrated the barley harvest in the spring. In other areas, they celebrated when new seeds were planted in the fall. New Year's was a particularly important festival and celebrated the marriage of the god Dumuzi to Inanna, filling the fields with abundance.

Ishtar, the goddess of love, was one of many Mesopotamian deities. This ivory plaque, thought to represent her, was found in the Assyrian palace at Nimrud.

EVERYDAY FOOD AND DRINK

Mesopotamians ate two meals a day. They relied heavily on barley for bread and beer. They also grew millet, wheat, rye, and rice. They made specialty breads mixed with fats and fruits. Fruits were plentiful. They included apples, pears, grapes, figs, quince, plums, apricots, cherries, mulberries, melons, and pomegranates. Mesopotamians made wine once a year with ripe grapes. Vegetables included lettuce, cabbage, radishes, beets, and turnips.

Onions, chickpeas, and lentils were also common ingredients in Mesopotamian food, especially soups.

Meat, though, was expensive. Animals were offered to the gods and the king. Mesopotamians ate mutton (sheep meat), goat, and beef. They raised chickens, geese, and ducks for their meat and eggs. They also ate fish and turtles.

To spice up their food, Mesopotamians used salt, coriander, cumin, mustard, fennel, marjoram, thyme, mint, and rosemary. To sweeten, they used grape and date juice. Only the rich could afford honey.

This stone cup decorated with bulls and ears of corn was used in Sumer around the fourth millennium BCE. It might have held beer or wine.

DAILY LIFE REMEMBERED

Much of what is known today about Mesopotamian daily life comes from archaeological finds. The Royal Tombs at Ur revealed Sumerian life of the third millennium BCE. There, archaeologists recovered elaborate headdresses and jewelry, wagons, and the remains of grains. Musical instruments were also found.

Ancient tablets depicted scenes of festivals, banquets, and wars. Narratives by travelers such as the Greek Herodotus also recorded their views of Mesopotamian daily life. *The Epic of Gilgamesh*, a long poem about the mythical king and hero, talks of everyday life. The Bible, too, adds to the knowledge, especially about the cities of Nineveh and Babylon.

Museums in America, the United Kingdom, Germany, France, and Iraq exhibit artifacts and tell the stories of the ancient civilizations that formed Mesopotamia. They remind visitors of the rich culture and beliefs of these ancient peoples and what their daily lives must have been like.

Excavations at the Royal Tombs at Ur recovered many significant relics of Mesopotamian daily life, such as this bull's head that belonged to a harp from the third millennium BCE.

GLOSSARY

agate A mineral with different-colored bands.
Amorites A group of Semites who came to Mesopotamia as soldiers and workers in the second millennium BCE.
amulets Small objects believed to have magic powers, worn to protect against evil spirits.
barter To exchange one good for another.
bitumen A substance used to waterproof ships and make roads.
carnelian A red gem imported from Africa and the Indus Valley.
chignons The arrangement of hair into small buns at the nape of the neck or on each side of the head.
concubines Women who live with the king but are not married to him.
epic A long poem that tells a story.
fortifications Walls built around cities to protect them from enemy attacks.
griffins Winged mythical creatures, whose likeness was often carved into furniture.
irrigation Man-made flow of water to land to grow crops.
kaunakes The Greek word for a kind of layered skirt made of wool.
kelek A kind of raft kept afloat by the use of goatskins.
lapis lazuli A deep blue mineral or gem.
nomads People who roamed from one place to another in search of grazing lands for their animals.
quince A hard yellowish fruit made into jellies.
rudders The parts of ships or boats that allow control of steering.
Semitic A group of peoples and languages that includes Akkadians, Amorites, Egyptians, Arabs, and Jews.
tablets Ancient clay pieces that contain writings or pictures.

FOR MORE INFORMATION

American Museum of Natural History
Central Park West at 79th Street
New York, NY 10024
(212) 769-5100
Website: http://www.amnh.org
The American Museum of Natural History relates the history of Mesopotamia to nature, the environment, and science.

California Museum of Ancient Art
PO Box 10515
Beverly Hills, CA 90213
(818) 762-5500
Website: http://www.cmaa-museum.org
This museum houses recovered artifacts from Assyria and Sumer. It was founded to give Southern Californians access to the roots of civilization.

Canadian Society for Mesopotamian Studies
c/o RIM Project
University of Toronto
4 Bancroft Avenue, 4th floor
Toronto, ON M5S 1C1
Canada
(416) 978-4531
E-mail: csms@chass.utoronto.ca
Website: http://projects.chass.utoronto.ca/csms/main.html
Founded in 1980, this society examines the literature, culture, and history of ancient Mesopotamia.

Metropolitan Museum of Art
1000 Fifth Avenue
New York, NY 10028
(212) 535-7710
Website: http://www.metmuseum.org
The Metropolitan Museum of Art is a major center for Near Eastern art, including rock reliefs and other artifacts.

Oriental Institute of the University of Chicago
1155 E. 58th St.
Chicago, IL 60637
(773) 702-9520
E-mail: oi-museum@uchicago.edu
Website: https://oi.uchicago.edu
Founded in 1919, the Oriental Institute has a goal of serving as the world's leading center for study of ancient Near Eastern civilizations.

WEBSITES

Because of the changing nature of Internet links, Rosen Publishing has developed an online list of websites related to the subject of this book. This site is updated regularly. Please use this link to access the list:

http://www.rosenlinks.com/SRFAC/mdaily

FOR FURTHER READING

Bryson, Bernarda. *Gilgamesh*. Sacramento, CA: Pied Piper Press, 2012.

Doeden, Matt. *Tools and Treasures of Ancient Mesopotamia*. Minneapolis, MN: Lerner Publishing Group, 2014.

Feinstein, Stephen. *Discovering Ancient Mesopotamia*. Berkeley Heights, NJ: Enslow Publishers, 2014.

Head, Tom. *Ancient Mesopotamia*. Minneapolis, MN: Essential Library/ABDO, 2014.

Hunter, Nick. *Daily Life in Ancient Sumer*. Chicago, IL: Heinemann Raintree/Capstone, 2015.

Lassieur, Allison. *Ancient Mesopotamia*. New York, NY: Children's Press, 2012.

Lockwood, Sebastian. *The Epic of Gilgamesh: A Storyteller's Version*. LumenArts, 2013. Audiobook.

Nardo, Don. *Life in Ancient Mesopotamia*. San Diego, CA: ReferencePoint, 2014.

Nardo, Don. *Mesopotamia*. North Mankato, MN: Compass Point, 2012.

Oakes, Lorna. *Hands-On History! Mesopotamia*. Leicester, England: Armadillo, 2013.

BIBLIOGRAPHY

Ascalone, Enrico. *Mesopotamia*. Trans. by Rosanna M. Gianmmanco Frongia. Berkeley, CA: University of California Press, 2005.

Bertman, Stephen. *Handbook to Life in Ancient Mesopotamia*. New York, NY: Facts on File, 2003.

Bottero, Jean. *Mesopotamia: Writing, Reasoning, and the Gods*. Trans. by Zainab Bahrani and Marc Van de Mieroop. Chicago, IL: University of Chicago Press, 1992.

Delaporte, L. *Mesopotamia: The Babylonian and Assyrian Civilization*. Trans. by V. Gordon Childe. New York, NY: Barnes & Noble, 1925, reprinted 1970.

Kriwaczek, Paul. *Babylon: Mesopotamia and the Birth of Civilization*. New York, NY: St. Martin's Press/Thomas Dunne Books, 2010.

Nemet-Nejat, Karen Rhea. *Daily Life in Ancient Mesopotamia*. Peabody, MA: Hendrickson, 1998.

Oppenheim, A. Leo. *Ancient Mesopotamia: Portrait of a Dead Civilization*. Chicago, IL: University of Chicago Press, 1964, 1977.

INDEX

ABOUT THE AUTHOR

Barbara Krasner is the author of more than fourteen books for young readers. She holds an MFA in writing for children and young adults from the Vermont College of Fine Arts and teaches creative writing and children's literature in New Jersey. She first became interested in the ancient world in the fourth grade.

PHOTO CREDITS

Cover, pp. 1, 23, 31, 37, 39 Werner Forman/Universal Images Group/Getty Images; p. 3 Tolga Tezcan/Shutterstock.com; p. 5 © Classic Image/Alamy Stock Photo; pp. 7, 11 ullstein bild/Getty Images; p. 9 DEA/A. De Gregorio/De Agostini/Getty Images; p. 13 Ancient Art and Architecture Collection Ltd./Bridgeman Images; p. 15 Kean Collection/Archive Photos/Getty Images; pp. 17, 19, 21, 25, 33, 35 Print Collector/Hulton Archive/Getty Images; p. 27 Science & Society Picture Library/Getty Images; p. 29 Fethi Belaid/AFP/Getty Images; p. 41 DEA/M. Carrieri/De Agostini/Getty Images; cover, p. 1 tower of babel graphic Santi0103/Shutterstock.com; back cover and interior pages background map Marzolino/Shutterstock.com; cover and interior pages background textures and patterns zffoto/Shutterstock.com, Elena Larina/Shutterstock.com, llaszlo/Shutterstock.com

Designer: Michael Moy; Editor: Heather Moore Niver; Photo Researcher: Heather Moore Niver